THE UKRAINE WAR ECONOMICS AND PROLIFERATION OF SALW IN AFRICA

Baudouin Ngah Akoh

Table of Content

INTRODUCTION

The repercussions of armed conflicts extend far beyond the borders of their immediate theatre. This statement becomes abundantly clear when examining the intricate relationship between the Ukraine war, the economics of conflict, and the proliferation of Small Arms and Light Weapons (SALW) in Africa. As warfare rages in one corner of the world, its effects ripple across oceans and continents, leaving lasting imprints on regions far removed from the initial battleground. The ongoing conflict in Ukraine is a poignant example of this phenomenon, with its economic ramifications reaching out to influence SALW trade and armed violence in Africa. This article explores the complex web of connections between the Ukraine war, its economic dimensions, and the proliferation of SALW in Africa. We aim to dissect the various contributing factors, their implications, and the urgent need for international cooperation and intervention to address the multifaceted challenges of this intercontinental entanglement. The paper has four main sections; the first is titled The Ukrainian War Economics and Implications for Africa; the second is Promoting Development over Arms in Africa; the third is Violent Extremists and Arms Trafficking in the Sahel; and the fourth and last section is the Urgent Need for a New Strategy to Combat SALW Proliferation.

The Ukrainian War Economics and Implications for Africa

Armed conflicts often lead to weapons proliferation and, following the conflict's conclusion, contribute to illegal arms distribution among criminal and insurgent groups in and around the affected regions. Given historical precedents, it is foreseeable that the Russia-Ukraine war may result in new weaponry sources for various actors, from insurgents in Africa to criminal organizations operating in European streets. Furthermore, Russia and Ukraine have well-established organized crime networks, forming a significant criminal ecosystem in Europe. These criminal entities operate transnationally, facilitating the smuggling of various commodities, including gold, timber, tobacco, coal, counterfeit or untaxed goods, humans, and drugs between Russia and Western Europe. Additionally, corrupt officials and criminal leaders exploited Ukraine's role as a transit point for Russian gas, resulting in substantial financial losses.

Moreover, the Russian invasion disrupted the collaboration between Russia and Ukraine in combating these crime risks (Galeotti & Arutunyan, 2023; Global Initiative Against Transnational Organized Crime, 2022; 2023:1,2).

Aside from Russia's invasion of Ukraine in 2022, Russia's political and military involvement in Africa has seen a noticeable increase as part of its strategy to expand its influence on the continent. Russia employs various means, including arms sales and the use of private military companies like the Wagner Group, which operates oppressively. This group has complex ties to political influence operations and economic entities, including mining companies. It is worth noting that the U.S. government has designated the Wagner Group as a 'transnational criminal organization' (Center for Strategic and International Studies, 2022; Vircoulon & Rademeyer, 2023; Mishra, 2023).

The War and Africa's Worsening Poverty

Russia and Ukraine, both significant exporters of wheat and sunflower, play critical roles in supplying these products to Africa. African countries largely rely on these imports, accounting for 80 percent of their wheat consumption (Vircoulon & Rademeyer, 2023; Mishra, 2023; Sacko & Mayaki, 2022; El Gomati, 2023). A recent UNDP study on the impact of the Ukraine war on sustainable development in Africa reveals a range of consequences influenced by factors such as oil and gas exports or imports, tourism, grain and fertilizer imports, and more. These effects disproportionately affect the most vulnerable populations, as a significant portion of their budget goes toward food and transportation. Food insecurity is expected to persist, negatively impacting income, health, and education (Lusigi, 2022). Additionally, Western sanctions on Russia will likely disrupt commercial flows between Russia and Africa, partly due to the closure of essential Black Sea ports. With Russia being a major global fertilizer exporter, concerns are growing about a potential worldwide fertilizer shortage, which could increase food prices and affect agricultural production and food security (Yohannes-Kassahun, 2023).

Furthermore, Russia ranks as the world's third-largest oil producer, and the disturbance in oil prices on the global market is expected to result in higher fuel prices and increased food production costs. Certain regions, including the Horn of Africa and the Sahel, face heightened food insecurity risks due to specific country-based shocks, climate change, export restrictions, and stockpiling. The ongoing conflict's impact on rising fertilizer and energy-intensive input costs may exacerbate the upcoming agricultural season (Sacko & Mayaki, 2022; El Gomati, 2023).

Turning Misfortune into Opportunity

Sacko and Mayaki (2022) and El Gomati (2023) outline how the economic implications of the Ukrainian war can be transformed into an opportunity for Africa's growth. Many African countries possess abundant agricultural and mineral resources. What is required is a concerted effort from African countries, the African Union (AU), the African Development Bank (AfDB), and regional economic groups to focus on innovative agriculture, promote intra-African trade, and harness the continent's potential. With 60 percent of the world's arable land, African countries can significantly increase food production for domestic consumption and global export, aligning with the AU's Agenda 2063 and the United Nations' Sustainable Development Goals (SDGs). Prioritizing agricultural and processing initiatives can prevent future disruptions across Africa's wheat, grains, and sunflower supply chain. Leveraging digital and biotechnologies for food system transformation is essential to support large-scale food production and transform African food systems (Ehui, 2018). African countries that produce these cereals and vegetable oils should enhance their capacity for production and supply, promoting intra-African trade and stimulating growth.

The African Continental Free Trade Area (AfCFTA) is identified as a game changer for Africa, with the potential to contribute significantly to a combined GDP of US$2.5 trillion; a substantial portion coming from the agribusiness sector. African countries should enhance their oil and gas production and exploration capabilities to safeguard against potential food price shocks resulting from global oil and gas price surges and reduce reliance on external sources. This approach can help stabilize fuel prices and lower food costs (Sacko & Mayaki, 2022; World Economic Forum, 2023).

Supportive Actions

Several supportive actions can help transform the challenges posed by the Ukrainian war into opportunities:

·   With support from development partners, African governments and institutions should prioritize building resilient food systems by supporting agricultural growth, enhancing farmer productivity, and deploying innovative technologies and financing in line with the AU's Comprehensive Africa Agriculture Development Program (CAADP) (AU, 2021).

·   The World Bank and International Monetary Fund should offer increased financial support to Africa, including funding, technical assistance, private sector participation, and investment, without pressuring African countries to adopt fiscal consolidation measures that could further raise food prices and social spending.

·   Stabilizing commodity markets, tackling debt burdens, enhancing capacity to cope with crises, and supporting green energy initiatives, in line with the U.N.'s

Global Crisis Response Group, should be prioritized.

·   Promoting inclusive structural transformation through digital advancements, cross-border collaboration, and removing non-tariff barriers to food trade, including reducing transportation costs and bureaucratic obstacles, is essential.

Overall, African countries should embrace the AfCFTA and promote open trade, reducing the need for imports from outside the continent where similar products can be produced effectively and efficiently (Global Response Group, 2023; Lusigi, 2022).

Promoting Development over Arms in Africa

Parachini and Bauer (2021) correctly assert that Africa truly needs development from Russia and other advanced countries, not more weaponry. Currently, Russia is the largest exporter of weapons to Sub-Saharan Africa, raising questions about the rationale behind arming a continent with vast economic potential. Moscow has significantly increased its presence in the African arms trade, maintaining a dominant position in the market (Kondratenko, 2020). To further its influence, Russia has cultivated ties with paramilitary groups such as the Wagner Group, often described as private military contractors (PMCs) with a more robust state affiliation than similar entities elsewhere (Khanyile, 2022; European Commission, n.d). The Wagner Group provides military training or protection to African leaders in exchange for fees and or access to mineral resources. However, the group has faced allegations of human rights abuses and worsening conflicts in its operational areas. U.N. peacekeepers have received reports of PMCs colluding with corrupt military officers in host countries, leading to grave violations (El Gomati, 2023; Kondratenko, 2020; Center for Strategic and International Studies, 2022).

African Union's "Silencing the Guns" Initiative

In 2020, the United Nations Office for Disarmament Affairs (UNODA) and the African Union Commission (AUC) jointly initiated a project to support African States in implementing Africa Amnesty Month. This project, funded by Japan and Germany, involved 13 African States in various phases. These States included Burkina Faso, Cameroon, the Central African Republic, Côte d'Ivoire, the Democratic Republic of the Congo, Ethiopia, and Kenya in 2020; Madagascar, Niger, and Uganda in 2021; and Liberia, Tanzania, and Togo in 2022. The Regional Centre on Small Arms (RECSA) collaborated to ensure regional and national engagement. National Focal Points and National Commissions responsible for small arms control played pivotal roles in implementing the project. In addition to the State's commitment to curbing unlawful gun ownership, Africa Amnesty Month allowed civilians to contribute to the 'Silencing the Guns' initiative by voluntarily surrendering illegally possessed firearms to national authorities (Nakamitsu & Lamamra, 2020).

Under the UN-AU collaborative project, beneficiary States launched extensive awareness campaigns emphasizing the dangers of illegal gun ownership and the illicit flow of small arms and light weapons. They also strengthened their capacities in stockpile management and community-based policing, ultimately collecting and publicly destroying weapons voluntarily surrendered by civilians. While the project's core activities were similar across the countries, each beneficiary State tailored its efforts to address specific national and regional contexts. As a result, more than 22,000 weapons were collected and destroyed across these 13 countries. The joint United Nations-African Union project will continue in the coming years (Nakamitsu & Lamamra, 2020).

Lessons from the U.S. Experience in Afghanistan

The U.S. withdrawal from Afghanistan in August 2021 inadvertently left behind a massive cache of small arms and light weapons (SALW) exceeding 650,000 pieces, including rifles and rocket-propelled weapons. Unlike sophisticated aircraft, SALW and MANIPODs require minimal training to operate effectively. Even newly recruited Taliban foot soldiers can handle an AK-47. This unintentional stockpile created a "regional arms marketplace" that benefits terrorists, criminal organizations, and insurgent groups. Similar situations have been observed in Libya and the past Russo-Ukrainian wars (Chavez & Swed, 2022). The collapse of a well-armed state triggers significant proliferation events, marked by a sudden surge in black market arms and their spread throughout the region (US, 2022)

The characteristics of SALW make them highly suitable for trafficking. They are small and modular, easy to conceal, ideal for transport through checkpoints and "ant-trade" routes, resembling the behavior of ants to avoid detection. They are durable and require minimal maintenance, making them cost-effective over time, with readily available parts and ammunition. The combination of weak governance, local incentives, and the nature of SALW facilitates their dispersion following a state's collapse. The consequences of this dispersion vary depending on the destination. In the case of Afghanistan, dispersion exacerbated instability in vulnerable regions, fueled insurgent efforts, strengthened existing terrorist organizations, created political vacuums for new groups to emerge, and even led to civil war. Specific outcomes depend on demand dynamics at trafficking endpoints (UN, 2021; Chaves & Swed, 2022).

Violent Extremists and Arms Trafficking in the Sahel

Arms trafficking in West Africa and the Sahel region has significantly contributed to armed conflicts, criminal activities, instability, and violent extremism. Violent extremist organizations (VEOs) like Jama'at Nasr al-Islam wal Muslimin (JNIM), the Islamic State (IS), and Boko Haram continually undermine regional military operations. VEOs frequently target communities, leading to a proliferation of arms in the region. As explained above, this proliferation is fueled by various sources (Nakamitsu & Lamamra, 2020). Despite efforts like the Declaration of Moratorium on Importation, Exportation, and Manufacture of Light Weapons in West Africa, intra-continental and intra-regional arms trade continues, perpetuating the illicit arms market. Seizures of SALWs by authorities offer insight into the volume of weapons in circulation. Arms trafficking is reinforced by illicit activities, such as drug and human trafficking and organized crime, rather than solely serving extremist groups or militias. Local and regional production and the looting of national stockpiles remain challenging to quantify but significantly contribute to arms trafficking in the Sahel. Strengthening anti-arms trafficking measures, enhancing regional cooperation, and addressing corruption are essential to countering arms trafficking in the Sahel and fostering long-term peace (UNODC 2023).

Addressing the Human Impact

Understanding the profound human toll of arms trafficking and proliferation in the Sahel is crucial to comprehend the urgency of addressing this issue. According to data from the Armed Conflict Location and Event Database spanning from February 2018 to February 2021, over 67,400 individuals lost their lives due to armed clashes, attacks, mob violence, or territorial disputes involving non-state or government actors in Mali, Niger, Nigeria, and Burkina Faso. Burkina Faso witnessed the sharpest increase in fatalities compared to Mali and Niger, with annual deaths rising from approximately 300 in 2018 to nearly 1,900 in 2019. Additionally, those affected by arms trafficking include people forcibly displaced due to escalating violence (UNODC 2023).

As of March 2021, the region counted 871,765 refugees and asylum seekers. Burkina Faso reported 1,097,462 internally-displaced persons (IDPs), Chad had 336,124 IDPs, Mali recorded 322,957 IDPs, and Niger had 298,458. These statistics underscore how small arms and light weapons (SALW) in the hands of various actors in the Sahel contribute to persistent violence. For instance, the threat from groups like Boko Haram has prompted many small villages to establish security forces or "vigilance committees" for self-protection. The prevalence of arms in the region has also exacerbated tensions between communities, such as farmers and herders in Nigeria, leading to an increased reliance on SALWs for dispute resolution and self-defense. Thus, curbing arms trafficking holds significant implications for individuals forced to engage in the illicit arms trade to safeguard themselves against destabilizing groups (UNODC 2023).

The border regions of Niger face a heightened risk of violence related to arms trafficking due to the relatively informal structures of these communities. In these remote areas, often beyond the reach of national government resources, arms trafficking intensifies the violence and radicalization. As citizens arm themselves against each other and security forces encroach on their lands, violent extremist groups move into these areas, capitalizing on the presence of armed individuals. Those who do not join these extremist groups may still engage in the illicit arms trade for survival and income. The livelihoods of local populations are partially impacted by influential figures who control various trafficking networks and routes in and out of Niger (UNODC 2023).

Additional underlying factors contributing to arms trafficking and proliferation in the Sahel include inadequate security infrastructure to combat illicit arms, poor border policing, insufficient funding for security personnel, and international actors who violate arms embargoes by arming violent groups. These factors create an environment where international actors like the United States and France have felt compelled to intervene based on international cooperation and national security interests. Despite arms seizures by French forces, international troops have done little to curb arms proliferation in the Sahel. It has provided minimal incentives for local and regional governments to allocate resources or reform amid ongoing conflict. These compounding issues affecting regional stability necessitate a comprehensive strategy to combat further proliferation by examining who is affected and how these individuals respond to illicit arms trafficking, ultimately forming a strategy to prevent future proliferation (UNODC 2023).

Challenges and Implications

The Sahel region is where Africa's major illicit SALW markets exist, with several illicit actors involved in arms trafficking and related criminal activities. For instance, private arms smuggled from Bulgaria, Ukraine, and Russia are exchanged for gold, diamonds, and other rare minerals mined in countries like Liberia, Togo, Nigeria, and Burkina Faso. Other illicit activities, such as human trafficking, drug trafficking, and wildlife trafficking, are facilitated by using or selling SALWs. Arms trafficking, in turn, finances extremist and criminal organizations in the Sahel. There are well-established traffickers with extensive smuggling networks that either bypass officials tasked with monitoring the import and export of goods or collaborate with security officials (Wenig, 2023; Jesse, 2023).

Nigerien, Chadian, and Nigerian officials have been accused of selling arms and ammunition from national stockpiles to extremist actors like Boko Haram. In Nigeria, it is reported that corrupt security officials "donate" or sell weapons to local groups involved in ethnic conflicts. Religious and ethnic motivations among security personnel can sometimes blur proper reasoning, especially as groups in conflict mix and trade weapons for various, sometimes conflicting, reasons. The active involvement of state officials in the illicit arms trade is mainly due to the near absence of state authority in violence-prone areas, allowing corrupt actors to operate with impunity. Even at the national/regional capitals, in nearly all the Sahel states, limited state capacity appears to be the norm. These countries host various fragmented illegal groups contesting power with the State, exploiting the limited state capacity, corruption, and the illicit arms markets in the region.

Even with strict monitoring and enforcement along the major border, arms looted from national stockpiles and military bases still fall into the hands of extremist groups and criminals due to weak governance capacity. Some national stockpiles have never had the infrastructure, funding, or personnel to manage a significant volume of weapons. Seized weapons are sometimes neither immediately destroyed nor deactivated and are not marked or traced according to international best practices for handling illicit weapons. National stockpiles are often overwhelmed by the number of weapons recovered from ongoing conflicts and criminal actors, forcing officials to establish makeshift storage areas. These ineffective procedures for managing seized weapons reflect the limited state capacity in the Sahel countries to handle their stockpiles. In effect, porous borders and low levels of policing facilitate the smuggling of SALWs across borders, especially in countries like Nigeria, which has over 1,500 irregular or illegal entry points. Therefore, addressing arms trafficking necessitates a comprehensive approach, including state-building, anti-corruption measures, and increased training for security forces. Thus, arms trafficking exacerbates conflict and perpetuates violence in the Sahel (Wenig, 2023; Jesse, 2023).

Efforts and Limitations

Amid the rapid proliferation of illicit arms in the past decade, governments in the Sahel and West Africa have made several attempts to address the issue and the resulting insecurity. For instance, in 2017, Burkina Faso, Mali, and Niger collaborated to establish a joint security force aimed at countering terrorism and transnational organized crime in the Liptako-Gourma region, covering southwestern Niger, eastern Mali, and northern Burkina Faso. Similarly, the G5 Sahel Joint Force, comprising Burkina Faso, Mali, Mauritania, Niger, and Nigeria, launched in 2017, continues to lead operations against extremist groups and criminal organizations.

Mali, in particular, has faced difficulties addressing ongoing violence, exacerbated by a coup in August 2020. Moreover, internal disputes over land and water resources have escalated, leading to deadly clashes, such as the March 2019 incident where 160 ethnic Fulani civilians were killed by armed individuals masquerading as ethnic Dogon hunters in central

Mali. These conflicts among numerous armed groups within Mali provide extremists with opportunities to exploit ethnic tensions and the State's inability to respond effectively to severe violence. Moreover, cooperating with non-state armed groups, such as the Self-Defense Group of Imrad Tuareg and Allies and the Movement for the Salvation of Azawad, which are simultaneously involved in other conflicts, has exacerbated inter-communal rivalries, territorial disputes, and arms proliferation in the Sahel. These efforts to negotiate with non-state armed groups and other counter-extremism initiatives have had little impact on the proliferation of SALWs in the region. The focus on resolving political disputes through negotiations and repelling extremist groups from border regions has not addressed corruption, weak state capacity, and short-term thinking within the security sector (Wenig, 2023; Jesse, 2023).

Causing significant constraint of immeasurable magnitude is the proliferation of shoulder-fired surface-to-air missiles, known as Man-Portable Air Defense Systems (MANPADS), which pose a risk to regional and international forces engaged in counterterrorism and security operations. It limits the potential for increased air support and threatens the continuity of these operations.

Addressing Corruption in the Sahel

Anti-corruption measures are critical to combat arms trafficking and proliferation in the Sahel. Burkina Faso, Mali, Niger, and Nigeria's governments must combat corruption and strengthen budgetary and anti-graft institutions. Corrupt authorities participating in the illicit arms economy should be prosecuted transparently to deter others from engaging in illegal arms deals. Civil society organizations can play a vital role in combating arms trafficking by holding authorities publicly accountable, advocating for good governance, and intensifying their whistle-blower role. Anti-corruption measures should improve the effectiveness and visibility of local and national police forces while incentivizing ethical behavior.

Additionally, courts should be well-funded and popularized as the preferred channel for resolving disputes related to territorial matters and corruption charges. Moreover, a more robust security apparatus throughout the Sahel will deter arms traffickers from operating in the region. Collaborative efforts that include reform like anti-corruption practices or efforts to prosecute and prevent human rights abuses by security forces may attract support from international stakeholders and donors. These partnerships can be built on shared intelligence, enabling governments to apprehend arms traffickers along well-known routes as they enter the region (Wenig, 2023).

Urgent Need for a New Strategy to Combat SALW Proliferation

The Task Force on Countering Extremism in the Fragile States was convened to tackle the escalating threat of extremism and explore more effective strategies for curbing the proliferation of Small Arms and Light Weapons (SALW). The move is necessary because of the sharp increase in terrorism since 2001. Extremism, driven by an ideology that seeks to establish totalitarian rule and dismantle free societies, underpins the surge in terrorism and armed violence worldwide. Prioritizing proactive prevention will protect societies and preserve peace, mainly if it includes strategic efforts to coordinate investments in high-risk areas. Through targeted, evidence-based strategies, prevention offers a cost-effective way to slow down and eventually reverse the spread of extremism. Fragile states and societies must take the lead in averting future extremist threats (Task Force on Extremism in Fragile States, 2019).

State Fragility, Extremism, and SALW Proliferation

The root cause of extremism and the proliferation of SALW is state fragility. Fragile states, characterized by weak governance, conflict, and political or religious grievances, are highly susceptible to extremist ideologies (US, 2019). Over 99% of deaths resulting from terrorist attacks in the past two decades occurred in conflict-ridden countries. Fragile states nurture extremism and become arenas for global power struggles. Nations like the US, France, Russia, China, and Iran exploit the instability in fragile regions to expand their influence. Extremism, authoritarian influence, and efforts to remove unpopular governments create self-perpetuating conflicts in these states, turning them into battlegrounds in the fight for freedom. If the aim is to address the root causes of extremism, a preventive approach should complement counterterrorism efforts, focusing on averting the emergence of extremism rather than just eliminating threats. For instance, leading powers can insist on free electoral processes rather than tacitly supporting unpopular governments, as seen in the coups in Niger and Gabon in 2023. Despite its challenges, a preventive approach is often the most cost-effective and realistic way to combat extremism in fragile states (Task Force on Extremism in Fragile States, 2019; World Bank, 2018).

Addressing Firearms Trafficking in the Sahel

In the Sahel region, a surge in firearms connects violent crime and conflict, blurring the lines between them. Armed groups engage in various forms of violent and criminal activities, and the region has experienced numerous periods of upheaval since the 1990s. Insurgency and banditry in the Sahel can be attributed to several factors, including inter-communal tensions, conflicts between herders and cultivators, religious extremism, and competition for resource control. The ongoing conflicts have led more individuals and communities to arm themselves. For the victims of violence, the motivation behind these actions matters little, whether they are driven by criminal or political motives (UNODC 2023).

The Fall of Libya and SALW Proliferation in the Sahel

The downfall of Libyan leader Muammar Gadhafi in 2011 significantly exacerbated instability in the Sahel. Tuareg soldiers who had served in the Libyan military returned to the Sahel with looted weapons, sparking a series of Tuareg rebellions in northern Mali. This rebellion was followed by a coup in Mali in 2012, creating a power vacuum exploited by extremist groups affiliated with Al Qaeda and the Islamic State. These extremist groups have continued destabilizing the region, leading to the expansion of the conflict into Burkina Faso and Niger, particularly in the transborder region known as Liptako-Gourma (UNODC 2023).

The Global Implications of Sahel's Vibrant Arms Markets

The Sahel region hosts vibrant black markets for firearms. The increasing number of bandits and traffickers competing for control of trade routes has driven the demand for firearms. Firearms trafficking in the Sahel involves long-range trafficking routes, including air routes from France and Turkey via Nigeria and regional procurement within Africa. Most firearms trafficked in the region come from Libya, diverted weapons from national militaries, legacy firearms from past conflicts, transfers from state security forces to vigilante groups, and artisanal production. It is crucial to recognize that arms trafficking in the Sahel has broader global implications, intersecting with other criminal activities and fueling conflicts that displace populations and disrupt communities throughout the region. Although the number of individuals primarily engaged in large-scale arms trafficking appears limited, firearms appear to be traded opportunistically based on shifts in supply and demand. For instance, traders involved in cross-border commerce may choose to transport weapons alongside other goods to increase their profits.

A Vicious Circle of Firearms Trafficking and Armed Violence in the Sahel

Firearms trafficking and conflict in the Sahel are interconnected, forming a vicious cycle. Conflict fuels firearms trafficking, as combatants, community militias, and even some states require weapons and ammunition. Arming militias inadvertently contributes to the pool of weapons that can be diverted to conflict actors. The primary beneficiaries of this cycle are the arms traffickers themselves. The weak law enforcement capacity in the Sahel countries exacerbates the situation, promoting a high level of impunity that allows militants and criminals to operate with relative freedom, intensifies tensions between communities, and facilitates firearms trafficking. UNODC (2023) recommends several measures to address this situation, including strengthening data collection and analysis, enhancing preventive measures, improving investigations and tracing, promoting international cooperation, and focusing on artisanal weapons. Artisanal weapons remain a significant concern in the Sahel.

CONCLUSION

The intertwining dynamics between the Ukraine war economics, and the proliferation of Small Arms and Light Weapons (SALW) in Africa present a deeply concerning and complex narrative. Our investigation has shed light on the enduring consequences of armed conflicts and their impact on regions far removed from the initial battleground. The economic dimensions of the Ukraine war, fueled by the global demand for food, rare metals, and arms, have inadvertently spurred the proliferation of SALW in African nations. This intercontinental entanglement has created a vicious cycle of violence, instability, and human suffering.

The evidence is stark, as we have witnessed a surge in SALW-related armed conflicts, exacerbating many African countries' already fragile political landscapes. This influx of weapons has fueled violence and contributed to an array of criminal activities, including terrorism, drug and human trafficking, and organized crime. As a result, the international community must confront the urgent need for comprehensive solutions that address the economic incentives driving arms trade and its subsequent fallout.

To break this cycle, international actors must strengthen anti-arms trafficking measures, enhance regional cooperation, and tackle corruption head-on. By bolstering the capacity of African nations to manage and secure their borders and supporting anti-corruption initiatives, the global stakeholders can help disrupt the flow of SALW, curbing their destructive impact. Furthermore, investing in the development and governance of fragile states is essential to prevent the emergence of extremism and political instability, thus reducing the demand for SALW.

In conclusion, the Ukraine war is a stark reminder of the far-reaching repercussions of contemporary armed conflicts. The lessons learned from the economic interplay between the Ukraine war and SALW proliferation in Africa underscore the need for a unified global effort to confront this challenge. Only through coordinated international action can we mitigate the devastating consequences of this intercontinental nexus and pave the way toward peace, stability, and prosperity for Ukraine and the African continent. Our collective responsibility is to act swiftly, for the stakes are high, and the cost of inaction is too great.

REFERENCES

African Union. (2021, February 22). The Comprehensive African Agricultural Development Programme (CAADP). https://au.int/en/articles/comprehensive-african-agricultural-development-programme

Center for Strategic and International Studies. (2022, September 15). Putin's Proxies: Examining Russia's Use of Private Military Companies. Congressional Testimony by C. Doxsee. https://www.csis.org/analysis/putins-proxies-examining-russias-use-private-military-companies

Chávez, K., & Swed, O. (2022, July 12). WEAK STATES AND LOOSE ARMS: LESSONS AND WARNINGS, FROM AFGHANISTAN TO UKRAINE. War on the Rocks. https://warontherocks.com/2022/07/weak-states-and-loose-arms-lessons-and-warnings-from-libya-to-ukraine/

El Gomati, A. (2023, July 27). Russia's Rhetoric-Reality Gap in Africa. Wilson Center. https://www.wilsoncenter.org/blog-post/russias-rhetoric-reality-gap-africa

European Commission. (n.d.). Sanctions adopted following Russia's military aggression against Ukraine. https://finance.ec.europa.eu/eu-and-world/sanctions-restrictive-measures/sanctions-adopted-following-russias-military-aggression-against-ukraine_en

Galeotti, M., & Arutunyan, A. (2023). The Russo-Ukrainian war and the illegal arms trade. Peace and proliferation. Global Initiative Against Transnational Organized Crime Research Report. Retrieved from https://globalinitiative.net/analysis/russia-ukraine-war-illegal-arms-trade/

Global Initiative Against Transnational Organized Crime. (2022). New front lines: Organized criminal economies in Ukraine in 2022.

https://globalinitiative.net/analysis/organized-criminal-economies-ukraine-2022/

Global Initiative Against Transnational Organized Crime. (2023). Peace and Proliferation: The Russo-Ukrainian War and the illegal arms trade [EN/UK]. Reliefweb. https://reliefweb.int/report/ukraine/peace-and-proliferation-russo-ukrainian-war-and-illegal-arms-trade-enuk

Global Initiative Against Transnational Organized Crime. (2023). The grey zone: Russia's military, mercenary, and criminal engagement in Africa. https://globalinitiative.net/analysis/russia-in-africa/

Global Response Group. (2023). Global Crisis Response Group on Food, Energy, and Finance. https://news.un.org/pages/global-crisis-response-group/

Jesse, G. (2023, July 12). Arms Trafficking: Fueling Conflict in the Sahel. The

International Affairs Review. https://www.iar-gwu.org/print-archive/ikjtfxf3n mqgd0np1ht10mvkfron6n-bykaf-ey3hc-rfbxp-dp te8-klmp4

Khanyile, M. B. (2022, March 27). Sanctions against Russia will affect arms sales to Africa: the risks and opportunities. The Conversation. https://theconversation.com/sanctions-against-ru ssia-will-affect-arms-sales-to-africa-the-risks-an d-opportunities-180038

Kondratenko, T. (2020, May 29). Why Russia exports arms to Africa. DW. https://www.dw.com/en/russian-arms-exports-to- africa-moscows-long-term-strategy/a-53596471

Lusigi, A. (2022, June 30). Africa and the Russia-Ukraine conflict: Seizing the opportunity in the crisis. Africa Renewal. https://www.un.org/africarenewal/magazine/afric a-and-russia-ukraine-conflict-seizing-opportunit y-crisis

Mishra, A. (2023, October). Russia's Low-Risk, High-Reward Strategy for its Return to Africa (ORF Issue Brief No. 666). Observer Research Foundation. https://www.orfonline.org/research/russias-low-risk-high-reward-strategy-for-its-return-to-africa/

Nakamitsu, I., & Lamamra, R. (2020, September). Africa Amnesty Month: UN-AU joint call for the surrender of illicit weapons. Africa Renewal. https://www.un.org/africarenewal/magazine/september-2020/amnesty-month-un-au-joint-call-surrender-illicit-weapons

Parachini, J. V., & Bauer, R. (2021, November 17). What Does Africa Need Most Now: Russian Arms Sales or Good Vaccines? [Commentary]. Rand. https://www.rand.org/blog/2021/11/what-does-africa-need-most-now-russian-arms-sales-or.html

UNODC. (2023). Firearms Trafficking in the Sahel: Transnational Organized Crime Threat Assessment. https://www.unodc.org/documents/data-and-anal

ysis/tocta_sahel/TOCTA_Sahel_firearms_2023.p
df

U.S. Department of State. (2022, April 1).
United States Strategy to Prevent Conflict
and Promote Stability.
https://www.state.gov/united-states-strategy-to-p
revent-conflict-and-promote-stability/

United Nations Security Council. (2021,
October 7). Rapid Spread of Small Arms,
Light Weapons Still Threatening World
Peace, Exacerbating Plight of Civilians in
Conflict Zones, Disarmament Chief Tells
Security Council. Reliefweb.
https://reliefweb.int/report/world/rapid-spread-s
mall-arms-light-weapons-still-threatening-world
-peace-exacerbating-plight.

United States Institute of Peace. (2019,
February). Preventing Extremism in Fragile
States: A New Approach [Final Report of the
Task Force on Extremism in Fragile States].
https://www.usip.org/sites/default/files/2019-02/
preventing-extremism-in-fragile-states-a-new-ap
proach.pdf

Wenig, M. (2023, October 11). Africa: The Quiet Battlefield for Global Power. The International Affairs Review. https://www.iar-gwu.org/blog/iar-web/africa-the-quiet

World Bank Group. (2018, March). Maximizing the Impact of the World Bank Group in Fragile and Conflict-Affected Situations. https://documents1.worldbank.org/curated/en/855631522172060313/pdf/124654-WP-PUBLIC-MaximizingImpactLowresFINAL.pdf"

www.ingramcontent.com/pod-product-compliance
Lightning Source LLC
Chambersburg PA
CBHW051856250726
48659CB00006B/2240